Building Resilient Education Systems: Navigating Crises and Shaping the Future

Chapter Contents:

This book provides a comprehensive exploration of crises in education and strategies for resilience, offering practical insights and guidance for educators, policymakers, and stakeholders seeking to navigate challenges and shape a brighter future for education.

Introduction:

In today's interconnected world, the intersection of education, health, and economics is more pronounced than ever before. The crisis at Basseterre High School (BHS) serves as a stark reminder of the profound impact that institutional challenges can have on the well-being of our children and the broader community. "Crisis Management in Education" explores the multifaceted dimensions of the BHS crisis, offering insights and strategies for navigating similar challenges in educational institutions worldwide. Through a lens of business, commerce, and economics, this book examines the ripple effects of the BHS crisis, underscoring the imperative of proactive and decisive action in safeguarding our children's future.

Why This Book?:

This book serves as a call to action for educators, policymakers, and stakeholders in the education sector. By dissecting the complexities of the BHS crisis and offering actionable solutions, it empowers readers to confront similar challenges in their own contexts. Grounded in real-world examples and best practices, "Crisis Management in Education" equips readers with the knowledge and tools needed to mitigate risks, foster resilience, and ensure the continuity of quality education for all.

For Whom is This Book?:

- Educators and school administrators seeking to proactively address institutional challenges and mitigate risks.
- Policymakers and government officials tasked with overseeing educational systems and ensuring the well-being of students.
- Parents and community members concerned about the health and safety of children in educational settings.
- Researchers and academics exploring the intersection of education, health, and economics in crisis contexts.

- The principles garnered in this book are scalable and applicable across multi-sector disciplines.

Chapter 1: Understanding the Basseterre High School Crisis: Unraveling the Complexities

In the heart of the Caribbean, in Saint Christopher and Nevis the old Basseterre High School (BHS) as it was then, stood as a pulsating and vibrant symbol of education and community life for decades.

Yet, beneath its facade of learning lies a crisis that threatened the very fabric of its existence. To truly comprehend the complexities of the BHS crisis, one must peel back the layers of institutional challenges, societal dynamics, and historical precedents that have converged to create this perfect storm.

At its core, the BHS crisis encompasses a myriad of interconnected issues, ranging from environmental hazards to governance failures, and societal inequalities. The discovery of Hydrogen sulfide on the school premises serves as a tangible manifestation of the environmental threats that surfaced then affecting students and staff. This toxic substance, with its characteristic odor of rotten eggs, posed an immediate health risk and underscored the urgent need for remedial action.

However, the crisis extends far beyond mere environmental hazards. It is symptomatic of broader systemic failures, including inadequate infrastructure, lack of oversight, and bureaucratic inertia. For years, the voices of concerned parents and educators have been drowned out by the deafening silence of institutional complacency. This chapter seeks to unravel these complexities, shedding light on the root causes of the crisis and its far-reaching implications.

In the Caribbean context, where educational institutions often serve as pillars of community cohesion, the BHS crisis strikes at the very heart of social fabric. The repercussions extended beyond the walls of the school, reverberating through neighborhoods and towns, casting a shadow of uncertainty over the future of our youth. It is a sobering reminder of the fragility of our educational systems and the urgent need for proactive intervention.

Proverbially, the BHS crisis serves as a canary in the coal mine—a warning sign of deeper systemic issues that demand attention. Just as the presence of a single canary signaled danger in the depths of a coal mine, so too does the presence of Hydrogen sulfide at BHS signal underlying threats to the well-being of our children and the integrity of our educational institutions.

To illustrate, consider the case of a student, Maria, or Teacher Jane who developed respiratory issues after prolonged exposure to Hydrogen sulfide at BHS. Their story is not unique. Across the Caribbean, countless students and teachers face similar health risks due to environmental hazards at their schools. Their plight serves as a poignant reminder of the human cost of institutional neglect—a cost that extends far beyond the confines of the classroom.

Yet, amidst the turmoil, there are glimmers of hope. Communities have rallied together, demanding accountability and advocating for change. From grassroots movements to legal challenges, the response to the BHS crisis exemplifies the resilience and determination of Caribbean citizens to safeguard the future of their children.

The BHS crisis is not merely an isolated incident but a symptom of broader systemic challenges facing educational institutions in the

Caribbean and beyond. By unraveling the complexities of this crisis, we gain a deeper understanding of the underlying issues at play and the urgent need for decisive action. As we navigate the turbulent waters ahead, let us heed the lessons of the BHS crisis and strive to build a future where every child has access to safe, equitable, and quality education—truly a cornerstone of our collective prosperity and well-being.

Chapter 2: The Economic Impact of Educational Disruption

As we continue our journey through the complexities of the Basseterre High School (BHS) crisis, it becomes increasingly clear that the consequences extend far beyond the walls of the classroom.

In Chapter 1, we delved into the environmental and social dimensions of the crisis, unraveling its intricacies and highlighting the urgent need for action. Now, we turn our attention to the economic implications of educational disruption, shedding light on the ripple effects that reverberate through communities and economies alike.

Imagine a community where education serves as the cornerstone of economic prosperity—a place where schools are not just centers of learning, but engines of growth and opportunity. In such communities, the disruption of education due to crises like the one at BHS can have profound and far-reaching consequences. But what exactly are these consequences, and how do they manifest in everyday life?

Let us first consider the immediate impact on students and families. With schools closed or operating under suboptimal conditions, students are deprived of vital learning opportunities, jeopardizing their academic progress and future prospects. For parents, the disruption of education poses a dual challenge—balancing work responsibilities with the added burden of childcare and educational support. In a region where economic stability is often precarious, the strain on families can be immense, leading to financial hardship and social dislocation.

But the economic impact of educational disruption extends beyond individual households—it permeates through the fabric of society, leaving no sector untouched. Take, for example, the labor market. As students' education is disrupted, the pipeline of skilled workers entering the workforce is disrupted as well. This can have long-term implications for economic growth and competitiveness, as businesses struggle to find qualified employees and the likelihood of stagnating innovation and creativity.

Moreover, the economic ramifications of educational disruption are not confined to the present—they reverberate into the future, shaping the trajectory of entire economies. Consider the case of Maria, the student from Chapter 1 who developed respiratory issues due to environmental hazards.

As her education is disrupted, her future earning potential is compromised, affecting not just her individual prosperity but the overall productivity and competitiveness of the economy.

But perhaps the most insidious aspect of the economic impact of educational disruption lies in its exacerbation of existing inequalities. In a region marked by stark disparities in access to quality education, crises like the one at BHS widen the gap between the haves and the have-nots, perpetuating cycles of poverty and exclusion. This, in turn, undermines social cohesion and hampers efforts to build a more equitable and inclusive society.

As we reflect on the economic impact of educational disruption, we are confronted with a sobering reality: the cost of inaction far outweighs the cost of proactive intervention. The longer we delay in addressing crises like the one that occurred at BHS.

The greater the economic toll on individuals, communities, and nations alike. But amidst the challenges lie opportunities for transformation and renewal. By investing in resilient and inclusive educational systems, we can not only mitigate the economic impact of disruption but also lay the foundation for a more prosperous and equitable future.

The economic impact of educational disruption is profound and multifaceted, with far-reaching consequences for individuals, communities, and economies. By understanding these impacts and their underlying drivers, we can better appreciate the urgency of addressing crises like the one at BHS and mobilize collective action to build a more resilient and inclusive educational ecosystem. As we embark on this journey, let us heed the lessons of the past and strive for a future where every child has access to the education they need to thrive and succeed.

Chapter 3: Risk Management in Education: Lessons from the BHS Experience

Having explored the economic ramifications of educational disruption in Chapter 2, we now turn our attention to the critical issue of risk management in education. In light of the Basseterre High School (BHS) crisis, it is imperative that we learn from this experience and take proactive measures to mitigate similar risks in educational institutions worldwide. But what exactly does risk management entail, and how can the lessons from the BHS experience inform our approach?

At its core, risk management in education involves identifying, assessing, and mitigating potential risks that could impact the safety, well-being, and academic progress of students and staff. It encompasses a range of strategies and protocols aimed at safeguarding educational environments and ensuring continuity of learning in the face of adversity. But how do we translate these principles into actionable strategies, particularly in the context of a crisis like the one at BHS?

One key lesson from the BHS experience is the importance of proactive risk assessment and mitigation. As we saw in Chapter 2, the consequences of educational disruption can be far-reaching and profound. By conducting comprehensive risk assessments, educational institutions can identify potential hazards, such as environmental pollutants or infrastructure deficiencies, before they escalate into a full-blown crisis. But how can we ensure that these risk assessments are thorough and effective?

Another lesson from the BHS experience is the need for clear communication and transparency in crisis situations. Effective risk management requires open channels of communication between stakeholders, including students, parents, educators, and government officials. By keeping stakeholders informed and engaged, educational institutions can foster trust and collaboration, enabling swift and coordinated responses to emerging risks.

Moreover, the BHS crisis underscores the importance of robust contingency planning and crisis response protocols. Educational institutions must have in place clear and actionable plans for responding to emergencies, whether they are environmental hazards, natural disasters, or public health crises. By rehearsing and refining these plans regularly, schools can minimize disruption and ensure the safety and well-being of students and staff. But what steps can educational institutions take to strengthen their contingency planning efforts?

In addition to proactive risk assessment and crisis response planning, effective risk management in education requires a culture of accountability and continuous improvement. Institutions must be willing to learn from past mistakes and adapt their policies and procedures in light of new information and emerging threats. By fostering a culture of resilience and adaptability, schools can better prepare themselves to navigate the uncertainties of an ever-changing world. But how can we cultivate such a culture within educational institutions?

As we reflect on the lessons from the BHS experience, it is clear that effective risk management in education is not a one-time endeavor but an ongoing process of vigilance and adaptation. By drawing on the insights gleaned from crisis situations like the one at BHS, educational institutions can strengthen their capacity to identify, assess, and mitigate risks, thereby safeguarding the well-being and academic success of their students and staff.

Risk management in education is a multifaceted and dynamic process that requires proactive planning, clear communication, and a commitment to continuous improvement. By learning from the lessons of the BHS experience and applying best practices in risk management, educational institutions can create safer, more resilient learning environments for all. As we move forward, let us heed the call to action and prioritize the safety and well-being of our students and staff above all else.

Chapter 4: Crisis Communication and Stakeholder Engagement

Building upon the lessons learned from risk management in education, we now delve into the critical aspects of crisis communication and stakeholder engagement. In the wake of the Basseterre High School (BHS) crisis, effective communication and engagement with stakeholders are paramount to navigate through uncertainty and foster trust and collaboration. But what exactly does effective crisis communication entail, and how can we ensure meaningful engagement with stakeholders in times of crisis?

Crisis communication is the process of delivering timely, accurate, and transparent information to stakeholders during a crisis. It requires clear and concise messaging that addresses the concerns and needs of all parties involved. In the context of the BHS crisis, effective communication could have mitigated confusion and anxiety among students, parents, educators, and the wider community.

One key aspect of crisis communication is the importance of transparency and honesty. In times of crisis, stakeholders crave information and reassurance.

By providing timely updates and being transparent about the situation at hand, educational institutions can build trust and credibility with their stakeholders. However, navigating the delicate balance between transparency and confidentiality can be challenging. How can educational institutions strike the right balance in their communication efforts?

Evidently, crisis communication requires a proactive and multi channeled approach. Educational institutions must leverage a variety of communication channels, deploying current social media platforms, email, websites, and traditional media, to reach different segments of their stakeholder base. By diversifying their communication channels, schools can ensure that their messages reach a wide audience and are accessible to all.

In addition to effective crisis communication, meaningful stakeholder engagement is essential for navigating through crises like the one at BHS. Stakeholders, including students, parents, educators, government officials, and community members, all have a vested interest in the safety and well-being of students and staff. By actively involving stakeholders in decision-making processes and soliciting their feedback and input, educational institutions can foster a sense of ownership and accountability. But how can schools ensure that their stakeholder engagement efforts are inclusive and participatory?

Effective stakeholder engagement requires a commitment to listening and responsiveness. Educational institutions must be willing to listen to the concerns and perspectives of stakeholders and take meaningful action in response. By demonstrating empathy, solidarity and responsiveness, schools can build stronger relationships with their stakeholders and foster a culture of trust and collaboration. But how can educational institutions ensure that their stakeholder engagement efforts are truly responsive and meaningful?

As we reflect on the importance of crisis communication and stakeholder engagement in navigating through crises like the one at BHS, it is clear that these efforts must be grounded in principles of transparency, honesty, and inclusivity. By prioritizing effective communication and meaningful engagement, educational institutions can build resilience and trust, thereby navigating through uncertainty and fostering a sense of unity and solidarity within their communities.

Crisis communication and stakeholder engagement are integral components of effective crisis management in education. By prioritizing transparency, honesty, and inclusivity in their communication efforts and actively involving stakeholders in decision-making processes, educational institutions can navigate through crises with resilience and unity. As we move forward, let us heed the lessons of the BHS crisis and strive for open and collaborative communication practices that prioritize the safety and well-being of all.

Chapter 5: Legal and Ethical Considerations in Crisis Management

As we continue our exploration of crisis management in the wake of the Basseterre High School (BHS) crisis, it is essential to examine the legal and ethical dimensions that underpin effective crisis response. In this chapter, we delve into the legal obligations and ethical responsibilities that educational institutions must navigate during times of crisis. How can schools ensure compliance with legal requirements while upholding ethical principles? What are the implications of legal and ethical considerations for crisis management in education?

First and foremost, educational institutions must adhere to legal obligations related to the safety and well-being of students and staff. This includes compliance with health and safety regulations, environmental standards, and duty of care obligations. In the case of the BHS crisis, were there any legal breaches related to environmental hazards or workplace safety that exacerbated the situation? How can schools ensure full compliance with relevant laws and regulations to prevent crises from escalating?

Furthermore, ethical considerations play a crucial role in crisis management, guiding decisions and actions in times of uncertainty. Educational institutions have a moral obligation to prioritize the safety and well-being of students and staff above all else. This requires making difficult decisions that may involve temporary closures, relocation of students, or changes to academic schedules. Moreover, transparency and honesty are fundamental ethical principles that must guide crisis communication efforts. Educational institutions have a duty to provide accurate and timely information to stakeholders, even when the situation is uncertain or evolving. How can schools ensure that their communication practices uphold ethical standards and foster trust and transparency among stakeholders?

In addition to legal and ethical obligations towards students and staff, educational institutions must also consider the broader impact of crises on the community and society at large. This includes potential legal liabilities stemming from harm or damage caused by the crisis, as well as ethical responsibilities to address systemic issues and prevent future occurrences. Academic institutions are required to navigate the complex legal and ethical landscape of crisis management while also addressing broader societal concerns.

In addition, crisis management in education must take into account the rights and interests of all stakeholders, including students, parents, educators, and the wider community. This requires a careful balancing of competing interests and priorities, with a focus on promoting fairness, equity, and justice for all. How can schools ensure that their crisis response efforts are inclusive and respectful of the diverse needs and perspectives of stakeholders?

As we reflect on the legal and ethical considerations in crisis management, it is essential to learn from the lessons of the BHS crisis and apply them to future scenarios. This requires a proactive approach to risk assessment, crisis communication, and stakeholder engagement, grounded in principles of transparency, honesty, and accountability. How can schools use the insights gained from past crises to inform their legal and ethical decision-making processes in the future?

In conclusion, legal and ethical considerations are integral components of crisis management in education, guiding decisions and actions in times of uncertainty.

By prioritizing compliance with legal obligations, upholding ethical principles, and considering the broader impact on stakeholders and society, educational institutions can navigate through crises with integrity and resilience. As we move forward, let us heed the lessons of the BHS crisis and strive for a more ethical and legally compliant approach to crisis management that prioritizes the safety and well-being of all.

Chapter 6: Business Continuity - Planning for Educational Institutions

The concept of business continuity planning emerges as a critical component of ensuring the resilience and sustainability of educational institutions. In this chapter, we delve into the principles and practices of business continuity planning for educational institutions, drawing insights from previous chapters and real-world examples to empower institutions towards greater preparedness and adaptability in times of crisis.

Business continuity planning involves the development of strategies and protocols to ensure the continued operation of essential functions and services during and after a crisis. For educational institutions like Basseterre High School (BHS), this means having robust plans in place to safeguard the safety, well-being, and academic progress of students and staff amidst disruptions. How can educational institutions effectively plan for continuity in the face of uncertainty?

One key aspect of business continuity planning is the identification and prioritization of critical functions and services. Educational institutions must assess their core functions, such as teaching and learning, student support services, and administrative operations, and determine the resources and infrastructure needed to sustain these functions during a crisis.

Strategic continuity planning requires the development of contingency plans and alternative strategies to address disruptions to normal operations. This may include implementing remote learning platforms, establishing communication protocols for remote work, and securing backup facilities, with effective redundancy systems and resources ready and available to be deployed at a moment's notice. By anticipating potential disruptions and proactively implementing mitigation measures, educational institutions can minimize the impact of crises on their operations. How can schools develop effective contingency plans to maintain continuity during crises?

Furthermore, business continuity planning involves fostering a culture of resilience and adaptability within educational institutions. This requires ongoing training and preparedness initiatives to ensure that staff are equipped with the knowledge and skills needed to respond effectively to crises. By empowering staff to act decisively and collaboratively in times of uncertainty, schools can enhance their capacity to weather crises and emerge stronger on the other side. Academic institutions therefore must seek to cultivate a culture of resilience and adaptability among staff and stakeholders.

In addition to internal preparedness efforts, business continuity planning also requires collaboration and coordination with external stakeholders, including government agencies, community organizations, and industry partners.

Educational institutions must establish partnerships and communication channels to facilitate information sharing, resource mobilization, and mutual support during crises. By leveraging the collective expertise and resources of external stakeholders, schools can enhance their resilience and effectiveness in crisis response. How can schools foster collaboration and coordination with external stakeholders to strengthen their business continuity planning efforts?

It is essential to learn from the experiences of institutions like BHS and apply those lessons to future scenarios. By prioritizing the identification of critical functions, developing robust contingency plans, fostering a culture of resilience, and collaborating with external stakeholders, schools can enhance their capacity to maintain continuity and thrive amidst uncertainty.

Strategic business continuity planning is a vital aspect of crisis management in education, ensuring the resilience and sustainability of educational institutions in the face of uncertainty. By prioritizing preparedness, adaptability, and collaboration, schools can navigate through crises with confidence and emerge stronger on the other side. As we move forward, let us heed the lessons of the past and embrace a proactive approach to business continuity planning that empowers educational institutions to thrive in an ever-changing world.

Chapter 7: Financial Resilience in the Face of Institutional Challenges

In the journey of navigating through institutional challenges, such as those faced by educational institutions like Basseterre High School (BHS), financial resilience emerges as a cornerstone for sustainability and growth. In this chapter, we explore the principles and practices of financial resilience in the face of institutional challenges, drawing insights from previous chapters and real-world examples to empower institutions towards greater stability and adaptability.

Financial resilience refers to the ability of an institution to withstand and recover from financial shocks and disruptions while maintaining its core functions and operations. For educational institutions like BHS, financial resilience is essential for ensuring the continued delivery of quality education and support services to students amidst challenges such as budget constraints, economic downturns, and unforeseen crises.

One key aspect of financial resilience is prudent financial management and planning. Educational institutions must adopt sound financial practices, including budgeting, forecasting, and risk assessment, and ensure that they are well-prepared to anticipate and mitigate financial risks.

By maintaining a robust financial foundation, institutions can weather economic uncertainties and fluctuations while remaining focused on their core mission of serving students. How can schools implement effective financial management practices to enhance their resilience?

In considering this, financial resilience requires diversification of revenue streams and sources of funding. Educational institutions must explore innovative approaches to revenue generation, such as fundraising campaigns, partnerships with industry stakeholders, and grant funding opportunities. By diversifying their revenue sources, schools can reduce their dependence on any single funding stream and enhance their ability to adapt to changing financial landscapes.

Another aspect of financial resilience involves prudent investment in infrastructure, technology, and human capital. Educational institutions must prioritize investments that enhance efficiency, effectiveness, and sustainability, while also preparing for future challenges and opportunities. By investing in the development of staff skills and capabilities, schools can empower their workforce to innovate and adapt to changing circumstances, thereby enhancing institutional resilience. How can schools strategically invest in infrastructure and human capital to bolster their financial resilience?

In addition to internal financial management and planning, financial resilience also requires collaboration and coordination with external stakeholders, including government agencies, donors, and community organizations.

Educational institutions must engage in transparent and open dialogue with external stakeholders to foster trust, collaboration, and mutual support. By building strong partnerships and alliances, schools can access additional resources, expertise, and opportunities to enhance their financial resilience.

As we reflect on the principles and practices of financial resilience in the face of institutional challenges, it is essential to learn from the experiences of institutions like BHS and apply those lessons to future scenarios.

Prioritizing these realities requires prudent financial management, diversification of revenue streams, strategic investments, and collaboration with external stakeholders, schools can enhance their capacity to withstand and overcome financial challenges.

Financial resilience is a vital aspect of institutional sustainability and growth, particularly in the face of challenges and uncertainties. By adopting sound financial practices, diversifying revenue sources, investing strategically, and fostering collaboration with external stakeholders, educational institutions can strengthen their financial position and ensure the continued delivery of quality education and support services to students. As we move forward, let us embrace a proactive approach to financial resilience that empowers institutions to thrive in an ever-changing landscape.

Chapter 8: The Role of Technology in Crisis Response and Recovery

In the ever-evolving landscape of crisis management, technology emerges as a powerful tool for facilitating effective response and recovery efforts. Building upon the foundation of financial resilience discussed in the previous chapter, this chapter explores the indispensable role of technology in crisis response and recovery, offering practical insights and suggestions for maximizing its potential in educational institutions like Basseterre High School (BHS).

Technology serves as a catalyst for enhancing communication, coordination, and collaboration during times of crisis. In the context of educational institutions, digital platforms and communication tools enable stakeholders to stay connected and informed, even in the face of physical separation. From virtual classrooms and online learning platforms to communication apps and social media channels, technology empowers schools to maintain continuity in education delivery and support services during disruptions.

How can educational institutions leverage technology to facilitate seamless communication and collaboration among students, staff, parents, and external stakeholders during crises?

Technology plays a crucial role in data management and decision-making during crisis response and recovery efforts. Digital tools and analytics platforms enable institutions to gather, analyze, and disseminate real-time data and insights, informing strategic decision-making and resource allocation. By harnessing the power of data-driven insights, schools can optimize their crisis response efforts, identify emerging trends and patterns, and adapt their strategies accordingly. Schools therefore, are required to use technology effectively to gather and analyze data to inform crisis response and recovery efforts.

The effective deployment of technology facilitates remote access to critical resources and services, enabling continuity of operations even in the absence of physical presence. Cloud-based storage solutions, remote access platforms, and digital collaboration tools empower staff to work and collaborate from anywhere, ensuring the uninterrupted delivery of essential services and support to students and stakeholders.

By embracing remote technologies, schools can minimize disruptions to their operations and maintain resilience in the face of crises. How can educational institutions harness technology to enable remote access to essential resources and services during crises?

In addition to facilitating crisis response efforts, technology plays a vital role in promoting resilience and adaptability in the aftermath of crises. Digital learning platforms and educational technologies enable schools to offer flexible and personalized learning experiences to students, catering to diverse needs and preferences. By embracing innovative teaching methods and digital resources, schools can empower students to continue their education journey and thrive in the face of adversity.

As we reflect on the role of technology in crisis response and recovery, it is essential to recognize the need for ongoing investment in digital infrastructure, training, and capacity-building. Educational institutions must prioritize the adoption of technology-enabled solutions and provide adequate support and training to staff and stakeholders to maximize their effectiveness. By investing in digital readiness and resilience, schools can enhance their ability to navigate through crises and emerge even stronger and better.

In this regard, technology serves as a powerful enabler of crisis response and recovery efforts in educational institutions, empowering stakeholders to stay connected, informed, and resilient in the face of adversity. By embracing technology-enabled solutions for communication, data management, remote access, and learning, schools can enhance their capacity to navigate through crises and ensure continuity in education delivery and support services. Traversing the perils of our times mandates that we collectively harness the full potential of technology to build a more resilient and adaptable education system that can thrive in an ever-changing world.

Chapter 9: Community Partnership and Collaborative Solutions

In the journey of crisis management and resilience-building, community partnerships and collaborative solutions emerge as essential pillars for fostering collective action and sustainable outcomes. Building upon the discussion of technology's role in crisis response and recovery in the previous chapter, this chapter explores the transformative power of community partnerships and collaborative approaches in addressing challenges faced by educational institutions like Basseterre High School (BHS).

Community partnerships bring together diverse stakeholders, including government agencies, non-profit organizations, businesses, residents of our communities, parents, and civic minded citizens to collectively address shared challenges and pursue common goals.

In the context of educational institutions, community partnerships offer opportunities for schools to leverage external expertise, resources, and support to enhance their resilience and effectiveness in crisis response and recovery. It therefore means that educational institutions should cultivate meaningful community partnerships to address challenges and promote resilience mechanisms.

Moreover, collaborative solutions involve the co-creation and implementation of initiatives and strategies that draw upon the collective wisdom, resources, and strengths of all stakeholders involved. By fostering collaboration and cooperation among stakeholders, schools can harness the synergistic power of collective actions to address complex challenges and achieve sustainable outcomes.

From joint planning and resource-sharing to collaborative problem-solving and innovation, collaborative solutions empower communities to create positive change and build resilience. This is a sure way to foster collaborative approaches so as to empower communities to address challenges and drive positive change.

Notably, community partnerships and collaborative solutions engenders a sense of ownership, engagement, and empowerment among stakeholders, leading to greater acceptance and support for initiatives and programs. By involving community members in decision-making processes and action planning, schools can ensure that solutions are relevant, inclusive, and responsive to the needs and aspirations of the community.

In addition to addressing immediate challenges, community partnerships and collaborative solutions also lay the foundation for long-term resilience and sustainability. By building trust, fostering relationships, and nurturing a culture of cooperation and reciprocity, schools can create enduring networks and mechanisms for collective action and problem-solving. As we see, community partnerships and collaborative solutions can contribute immensely to long-term resilience and sustainability in educational institutions.

Considering the transformative potential of community partnerships and collaborative solutions, it is essential to draw upon lessons from previous chapters and real-world examples to inform our understanding and practices.

From the role of technology in facilitating communication and collaboration to the principles of financial resilience and crisis management, each aspect of our discussion contributes to a holistic approach to building resilience in educational institutions. This process facilitates a meaningful way of integrating community partnerships and collaborative solutions into our broader strategy for resilience-building.

Community partnerships and collaborative solutions offer a powerful framework for addressing challenges, promoting resilience, and driving positive change in educational institutions and communities.

This is achieved by fostering meaningful relationships, engaging stakeholders, and working together towards common goals. Schools can leverage the collective strength and wisdom of their communities to navigate through crises and emerge stronger on the other side. It is critical that we embrace the transformative potential of community partnerships and collaborative solutions to create a more resilient and equitable future.

Chapter 10: Lessons from Global Crisis Management Frameworks

Drawing from the foundational principles of community partnerships and collaborative solutions discussed in the previous chapter, we turn our attention to lessons gleaned from global crisis management frameworks.

In this chapter, we delve into insightful, practical, and relatable understandings derived from global perspectives on crisis management, exploring how these lessons can inform and enrich the resilience-building efforts of educational institutions like Basseterre High School (BHS).

One key lesson from global crisis management frameworks is the importance of proactive planning and preparedness. Global crises, such as the COVID-19 pandemic, have underscored the critical need for institutions to anticipate and mitigate risks before they escalate into full-blown emergencies.

In doing so, it is necessary to adopt a proactive approach to crisis management, schools can identify vulnerabilities, develop contingency plans, and build adaptive capacity to respond effectively to unforeseen challenges.

Furthermore, global crisis management frameworks emphasize the significance of collaboration and coordination across sectors and stakeholders. In an interconnected world, crises often transcend organizational boundaries and require coordinated responses from multiple actors.

By fostering collaboration among government agencies, non-profit organizations, businesses, and community groups, schools can harness collective expertise, resources, and support to address complex challenges and promote resilience. Educational institutions must then foster cross-sectoral collaboration and coordination in crisis response and recovery efforts.

Moreover, global crisis management frameworks highlight the importance of communication and transparency in building trust and resilience. Effective communication is essential for keeping stakeholders informed, engaged, and empowered during times of crisis. By establishing clear communication channels, disseminating accurate information, and soliciting feedback from stakeholders, schools can build trust, foster resilience, and mitigate the spread of misinformation and panic.

Additionally, global crisis management frameworks underscore the need for continuous learning and adaptation in the face of evolving threats and challenges. Crises are dynamic, frenetic and unpredictable, requiring institutions to remain agile, flexible, and open to innovation. By embracing a culture of continuous improvement and learning, schools can identify lessons learned from past experiences, incorporate best practices from global counterparts, and adapt their strategies to changing circumstances.

As we reflect on the lessons from global crisis management frameworks, it is essential to consider their relevance and applicability within the context of BHS and similar educational institutions. From proactive planning and cross-sectoral collaboration to effective communication and continuous learning.

Each lesson offers valuable insights and strategies for enhancing resilience and promoting positive outcomes. All stakeholders should endeavor to leverage these lessons to strengthen the crisis management capabilities of educational institutions.

Lessons from global crisis management frameworks provide invaluable guidance and inspiration for educational institutions seeking to build resilience and navigate through challenges effectively. By embracing proactive planning, collaboration, communication, and continuous learning, schools can enhance their capacity to withstand and overcome crises while fostering trust, resilience, and empowerment among stakeholders. As we embark on our journey towards greater resilience, let us draw upon these lessons to create a safer, more resilient future for all.

Chapter 11: Case Studies in Effective Crisis Management

As we delve deeper into our exploration of crisis management, it is invaluable to examine real-world case studies that demonstrate effective strategies and practices. Drawing upon insights from previous chapters and issues discussed, this chapter explores practical, insightful, and scientifically backed case studies in effective crisis management, offering practical solutions and lessons for educational institutions like Basseterre High School (BHS) and beyond.

One compelling case study is the response to the COVID-19 pandemic in South Korea. Through a combination of proactive testing, contact tracing, and quarantine measures, South Korea effectively contained the spread of the virus and minimized its impact on public health and the economy. By leveraging technology, data analytics, and community partnerships, South Korea demonstrated the power of a comprehensive and coordinated approach to crisis management.

Another noteworthy case study is the crisis management response to the Ebola outbreak in West Africa. Despite facing significant challenges and obstacles, including limited resources and infrastructure, local communities, international organizations, and governments collaborated to contain the spread of the virus and provide essential medical care to affected populations.

Through community engagement, communication, and targeted interventions, stakeholders successfully mitigated the impact of the Ebola outbreak and saved countless lives. How can educational institutions learn from the collaborative efforts and resilience demonstrated during the Ebola crisis?

The response to natural disasters, such as hurricanes, frequent storms, earthquakes, wildfires and so on provides valuable insights into effective crisis management practices. From pre-disaster preparedness and risk mitigation to post-disaster recovery and rebuilding efforts, communities around the world have implemented innovative strategies to address the multifaceted challenges posed by natural disasters.

In adopting a holistic approach that incorporates early warning systems, evacuation plans, and community resilience-building initiatives, stakeholders can minimize the human and economic toll of natural disasters and promote long-term sustainability. Educational institutions can incorporate lessons from natural disaster responses into their crisis management plans.

Moreover, case studies in organizational crisis management, such as product recalls, data breaches, and workplace accidents, offer practical insights into effective risk assessment, communication, and mitigation strategies. By studying successful examples of crisis management in various industries, educational institutions can identify best practices and develop tailored solutions to address their unique challenges and vulnerabilities. Academic institutions are now positioned to leverage insights from organizational crisis management case studies to enhance their own crisis preparedness and response capabilities.

It is essential, therefore, to consider their relevance and applicability within the context of the BHS crisis and similar educational institutions. From the COVID-19 pandemic to natural disasters and organizational crises, each case study offers valuable lessons and strategies for building resilience and promoting positive outcomes.

Case studies in effective crisis management provide valuable guidance and inspiration for educational institutions seeking to navigate through challenges and uncertainties. By studying real-world examples, learning from past experiences, and collaborating with stakeholders, schools can enhance their capacity to respond effectively to crises while fostering trust, resilience, and empowerment among their communities. As we apply the lessons learned from these case studies, let us strive to create a safer, more resilient future for all.

Chapter 12: Leadership in Times of Crisis: Navigating Uncertainty with Resolve

In times of crisis, effective leadership plays a pivotal role in guiding individuals and organizations through uncertainty with resilience and determination. Building upon the insights gleaned from previous chapters, this chapter explores the essential qualities, strategies, and practices of leadership in times of crisis, offering practical, reflective, and implementational understanding to navigate uncertainty with resolve in everyday life and living.

Effective leadership in times of crisis requires a combination of vision, empathy, decisiveness, and adaptability. Leaders must inspire confidence, provide clarity, and foster a sense of unity and purpose among their teams and communities. By articulating a clear vision for the future, empathizing with the challenges faced by stakeholders, making informed and timely decisions, and adapting to changing circumstances, leaders must instill trust and confidence in those they lead.

Moreover, leaders must communicate effectively and transparently with stakeholders, keeping them informed, engaged, and empowered throughout the crisis. Clear, honest, and empathetic communication builds trust, fosters collaboration, and mitigates the spread of misinformation, disinformation and fear. By actively listening to the concerns and perspectives of others, soliciting feedback, and providing regular updates on the situation, leaders can create a sense of stability and confidence in times of uncertainty.

Furthermore, effective leadership in times of crisis involves strategic decision-making and risk management to navigate complex and unpredictable challenges. Leaders must assess risks, weigh trade-offs, and prioritize actions based on their potential impact and likelihood of success. By taking a proactive and adaptive approach to crisis management, leaders can anticipate challenges, identify opportunities, and mobilize resources to address them effectively.

Poignantly, leaders must demonstrate resilience, optimism, and perseverance in the face of adversity, inspiring hope and confidence in others.

It is essential that they remain calm, composed, and solution-oriented, even in the most challenging circumstances, leaders can instill a sense of resilience and determination in their teams and communities. Drawing strength from their values, purpose, and sense of duty, leaders can navigate uncertainty with resolve and lead by example.

As we reflect on the qualities, strategies, and practices of leadership in times of crisis, it is essential to draw upon the lessons and insights from previous chapters to inform our understanding and approach.

From proactive planning and collaboration to effective communication and continuous learning, each aspect of our discussion contributes to a holistic understanding of leadership in times of crisis. We are encouraged to apply these insights and principles to become more effective leaders in our own lives, roles and responsibilities.

Unwavering and compassionate leadership in times of crisis requires vision, empathy, decisiveness, adaptability, effective communication, strategic decision-making, and foresight. By embodying these qualities and practices, individuals can navigate uncertainty with resolve and guide their teams and communities towards positive outcomes.

As we strive to become better leaders in times of crisis, let us draw upon these insights and principles to inspire hope, foster resilience, and create a brighter future for those in our circle of influence.

Chapter 13: Addressing Inquiries and Vulnerabilities in the Education System

How can we ensure the resilience and efficacy of our education systems in the face of uncertainties and vulnerabilities?.

This chapter delves into the critical importance of addressing inquiries and vulnerabilities within the education system, providing insightful, practical, and scientifically based information to guide stakeholders in navigating challenges and fostering a more robust educational framework.

One of the fundamental aspects of addressing inquiries and vulnerabilities in the education system is promoting transparency and accountability. Stakeholders, including educators, administrators, parents, and students, must have access to accurate and up-to-date information about the policies, practices, and performance of educational institutions.

By fostering a culture of openness and accountability, we can identify and address potential vulnerabilities, build trust, and enhance the overall integrity of the education system. How can we promote transparency and accountability in our educational institutions?

In addressing this issue, inquiries and vulnerabilities in the education system require a proactive approach to identifying and mitigating risks. This includes conducting thorough assessments of potential threats, such as environmental hazards, social inequalities, academic disparities, and technological disruptions, and implementing targeted interventions to minimize their impact. By fostering a culture of risk awareness and preparedness, we can better anticipate challenges, mitigate their effects and impacts, and safeguard the well-being and success of all learners. What steps can educational institutions take to proactively identify and address potential vulnerabilities?

Furthermore, addressing inquiries and vulnerabilities in the education system necessitates a comprehensive understanding of the diverse needs and experiences of students. This includes recognizing and focusing on systemic barriers hindering access to education in an equitable manner, in that way, seeking to eliminate or manage socioeconomic disparities, cultural differences, learning disabilities, and mental health challenges.

In promoting inclusive policies and practices that prioritize the needs of marginalized and underserved cross-section of the populations, we can create a more equitable and supportive learning environment for all students. It is necessary therefore to ensure that educational systems are inclusive and accessible to diverse learners.

Guided by these principles, constructive sightedness is needed in addressing inquiries and vulnerabilities in the education system which requires a commitment to continuous improvement and innovation.

This involves leveraging data-driven insights, evidence-based practices, and emerging technologies to enhance teaching and learning outcomes, promote student engagement and motivation, and the need to adapt to evolving educational needs and priorities. By embracing a culture of innovation and adaptation, we can overcome challenges, seize opportunities, and drive positive change within the education system. Educators and policymakers must work assiduosly to foster a culture of continuous improvement and innovation in education.

As we reflect on the significance and practical examples of addressing inquiries and vulnerabilities in the education system, it is essential to recognize that the resilience and effectiveness of our educational institutions depend on collaborative efforts and collective responsibility. By engaging stakeholders in meaningful dialogue, soliciting feedback, and prioritizing the well-being and success of all learners, we can create a more responsive, adaptable and equitable education system that empowers individuals to thrive in an increasingly complex and uncertain world.

It is incumbent on us all to work together to address inquiries and vulnerabilities in the education system and ensure the success of future generations.

In conclusion, addressing inquiries and vulnerabilities in the education system requires a multifaceted approach that prioritizes transparency, accountability, risk management, inclusivity, innovation, and collaboration. It is essential that we embrace these principles and practices, in order to build out a more resilient, equitable, and effective education system that empowers individuals to realize their full potential and contribute meaningfully to society.

Chapter 14: Preparing for Future Challenges: Building Resilient Educational Ecosystems

Gazing ahead, it is imperative that we equip our educational ecosystems with the resilience and adaptability needed to navigate the uncertainties and complexities ahead.

This chapter delves into the practical strategies, insightful examples, and scientific principles underlying the preparation for future challenges and the cultivation of resilient educational ecosystems. Drawing from the lessons and insights gleaned from previous chapters, we explore how stakeholders can collaborate to build a more robust and responsive educational framework that empowers learners to thrive in a rapidly changing world.

One of the key principles in preparing for future challenges and building resilient educational ecosystems is fostering a culture of innovation and adaptability. Educational institutions must embrace emerging technologies, pedagogical approaches, and organizational practices that enable them to respond effectively to evolving needs and priorities. By promoting a spirit of experimentation, creativity, and continuous improvement, we can cultivate a dynamic and forward-thinking educational ecosystem that is better equipped to address the challenges and opportunities of tomorrow.

Preparing for future challenges requires a proactive approach in identifying and addressing emerging trends and risks. This includes conducting thorough assessments of technological advancements, demographic shifts, economic fluctuations, environmental changes, and geopolitical developments that may impact the education sector.

If stakeholders in the education ecosystem remain informed and vigilant, they are better positioned to anticipate challenges, seize opportunities, and proactively adapt their strategies and practices to ensure the resilience and sustainability of their ecosystems.

This can be achieved by building resilient educational ecosystems that entails fostering strong partnerships and collaborations across sectors and disciplines. By engaging strategically with government agencies, industry partners, community organizations, and other stakeholders, educational institutions can leverage collective expertise, resources, and networks to address complex challenges and achieve shared goals.

Collaborative initiatives, such as public-private partnerships, leveraging and or monetizing intellectual property rights, research consortia, and community outreach programs, these systems can enhance the capacity of educational ecosystems to innovate, adapt, and thrive in an increasingly interconnected and interdependent world.

As a matter of first priority, preparing for future challenges requires a commitment to equitable organizational frameworks, inclusion, and social justice within educational ecosystems.

A significant part of the process must force our hands to address the faults of systemic barriers to access, participation, and success.

Educational institutions can ensure that all learners have the opportunity to reach their full potential, regardless of their background or circumstances. This may involve implementing targeted interventions, such as bespoke scholarship programs, the development of a business sports program, mentorship initiatives, and support services, to level the playing field and promote equitable outcomes for all students.

As we reflect on the principles and practices of preparing for future challenges and building resilient educational ecosystems, it is essential to recognize that the success of these efforts depends on collective action and shared responsibility.

By fostering a culture of collaboration, innovation, equity, and inclusion, educational stakeholders can create a more resilient, responsive, and sustainable ecosystem that empowers learners to thrive in an ever-changing world.

Preparing for future challenges and building resilient educational ecosystems requires a multifaceted approach that prioritizes innovation, foresight, collaboration, equity, and inclusion.

Therefore care must be taken in embracing these principles and practices, so that educational stakeholders can create a more adaptive, responsive, and empowering ecosystem that prepares learners for the opportunities and challenges of tomorrow.

As we embark on this journey towards a more resilient future, let us remain committed to working together to build a brighter and more inclusive world through education.

Chapter 15: Moving Forward Towards a Brighter Future for Education

As we forge ahead , it is essential to reflect on the insights and lessons learned from our exploration of the challenges and opportunities facing educational ecosystems.

In chapter 1 to 14, we have examined the complexities of crises, the economic impacts of disruption, the importance of risk management, crisis communication, legal and ethical considerations, business continuity planning, financial resilience, technological integration, community partnerships, global frameworks, effective case studies, leadership principles, and addressing vulnerabilities.

Now, as we transition to Chapter 15, let us synthesize these learnings and chart a path forward towards a more resilient, equitable, and innovative education system.

Throughout our journey, we have encountered a myriad of challenges, from environmental hazards to socioeconomic disparities, from technological disruptions to geopolitical uncertainties. Yet, amidst these challenges, we have also witnessed the resilience, creativity, and determination of educational stakeholders to overcome obstacles and seize opportunities for positive change. How can we harness these strengths to propel us forward towards a brighter future for education?

One of the key themes that emerged from our exploration is the importance of collaboration and partnership in addressing complex challenges.

We must continue to foster strong relationships and alliances across sectors, disciplines, and communities to build a more interconnected and interdependent educational ecosystem. It means therefore that we must leverage collective expertise, resources, and networks to create synergistic solutions that benefit all learners.

Moreover, our journey has underscored the critical role of innovation and adaptation in responding to evolving needs and priorities. As we navigate the uncertainties of the future, we must embrace emerging technologies, pedagogical approaches, and organizational practices that enable us to meet the diverse needs and aspirations of learners. It is imperative that we cultivate a culture of innovation and experimentation that fosters creativity, resilience, and lifelong learning.

Furthermore, our exploration has highlighted the importance of equity, inclusion, and social justice in creating a more just and equitable education system. As we strive towards a brighter future, we must redouble our efforts to dismantle all forms of systemic barriers which have stymied aggressive change in sustained quality outputs.

To this end, collectively, we must provide a guarantee that all learners have the opportunity to thrive, by eradicating systems that promote seclusion over inclusion, one pronged approach as opposed to diversity, and inequity over equity.

Additionally, our journey has emphasized the importance of foresight and preparedness in anticipating and mitigating future challenges.

We must remain vigilant and proactive in identifying emerging trends, risks, and opportunities, and developing strategies and interventions to address them effectively.

Let us draw inspiration from the insights and lessons learned from our exploration. By embracing collaboration, innovation, equity, and foresight, we can build a more resilient, inclusive, and transformative education system that empowers learners to thrive in a rapidly changing world.

Together, let us seize the opportunities before us and create a future where every individual has the opportunity to realize their full potential and contribute meaningfully to society.

We are mindful of the words of Nelson Mandela: "Education is *one of the* most powerful weapons which you can use to change the world." As we move forward, let us harness the power of education to build a brighter, more just, and more sustainable future for all.

Recap Summary:

In our journey through the chapters of this book, we have embarked on a comprehensive exploration of the challenges, opportunities, and strategies for building a brighter future for education. From understanding the crisis at Basseterre High School (BHS) to envisioning resilient educational ecosystems, each chapter has provided valuable insights and practical guidance for readers seeking to navigate the complexities of the education landscape.

Considerations for Readers:

Understanding Crisis Dynamics: Readers will gain a deep understanding of the multifaceted nature of crises in educational institutions, including the environmental, health, and social factors that contribute to their complexity. How can we proactively identify and mitigate potential crises before they escalate?

Economic Impacts of Disruption: By exploring the economic consequences of educational disruption, readers will recognize the far-reaching effects of crises on individuals, communities, and economies. How can we build financial resilience and adaptability into educational systems to minimize these impacts?

Risk Management Strategies: Through an examination of risk management principles, readers will learn how to anticipate, assess, and address risks effectively, thereby enhancing the safety and security of educational environments. What proactive measures can educational leaders take to mitigate potential risks?

Effective Crisis Communication: By delving into the importance of crisis communication and stakeholder engagement, readers will discover strategies for fostering transparency, trust, and collaboration during times of uncertainty. How can effective communication practices strengthen resilience and build community resilience?

Legal and Ethical Considerations: Through an exploration of legal and ethical dimensions of crisis management, readers will gain insight into the rights, responsibilities, and obligations of educational stakeholders in ensuring the safety and well-being of learners. What ethical dilemmas arise in crisis situations, and how can they be navigated?

Innovation and Adaptation: By examining the role of technology, innovation, and business continuity planning in crisis response and recovery, readers will discover opportunities for leveraging emerging tools and strategies to enhance educational resilience and effectiveness. How can technological advancements support learning continuity and adaptability?

Leadership and Collaboration: Reflections on leadership principles, community partnerships, and global frameworks for crisis management, readers will be inspired to cultivate leadership qualities and collaborative networks that promote collective action and positive change. What leadership qualities are essential for navigating uncertainty and fostering resilience in educational settings?

As readers engage with the insights and reflections presented in this book, they are invited to consider their own roles and responsibilities in shaping the future of education. By embracing innovation, collaboration, and resilience, we can work together to build a more equitable, inclusive, and sustainable educational ecosystem for generations to come.